THE PRACTICAL STRATEGIES SERIES IN GIFTED EDUCATION

series editors
FRANCES A. KARNES & KRISTEN R. STEPHENS

Acceleration Strategies for Teaching Gifted Learners

Joyce VanTassel-Baska

Routledge
Taylor & Francis Group
NEW YORK AND LONDON

First published 2005 by Prufrock Press Inc.

Published 2021 by Routledge
605 Third Avenue, New York, NY 10017
2 Park Square, Milton Park, Abingdon, Oxon OX14 4RN

Routledge is an imprint of the Taylor & Francis Group, an informa business

ISBN 13: 978-1-59363-014-0 (pbk)

Contents

Series Preface 1

Introduction 3

Review of the Research 4

Myths About Acceleration 7

The Perceived Effects of Acceleration 10

Acceleration Options 13

The Relationship Between Acceleration and Enrichment 17

Characteristics of Potential Accelerants 19

Curricular Emphases for Accelerated Study in Reading and Math 23

Strategies for Acceleration in Classrooms 27

An Acceleration Case Study 46

Organizational Necessities to Meet Gifted Students' Needs 50

Who Can Work With Accelerated Learners? 53

Making Acceleration a Useful Option 56

Responsible School Decision Making: Policy Recommendations 58

Conclusion 60

Resources 61

- Mathematics 61
- Social Studies 62
- Language Arts 62
- Science 62

References 64

Series Preface

The Practical Strategies Series in Gifted Education offers teachers, counselors, administrators, parents, and other interested parties with up-to-date instructional techniques and information on a variety of issues pertinent to the field of gifted education. Each guide addresses a focused topic and is written by scholars with authority on the issue. Several guides have been published. Among the titles are:

- *Acceleration Strategies for Teaching Gifted Learners*
- *Curriculum Compacting: An Easy Start to Differentiating for High-Potential Students*
- *Enrichment Opportunities for Gifted Learners*
- *Independent Study for Gifted Learners*
- *Motivating Gifted Students*
- *Questioning Strategies for Teaching the Gifted*
- *Social & Emotional Teaching Strategies*
- *Using Media & Technology With Gifted Learners*

For a current listing of available guides within the series, please contact Prufrock Press at (800) 998-2208 or visit http://www.prufrock.com.

Introduction

The acceleration of gifted children and their curriculum is a necessary first step in appropriate provisions for them. While many strategies are successful with the gifted, none surpass acceleration's efficiency and effectiveness in promoting long-term learning in the gifted and eliminating boredom and mental laziness. As an intervention for gifted learners, however, it has been underutilized due to misconceptions and its lack of fit with school curricular organizational patterns. Yet, there are several teacher-friendly ways the process of acceleration can be employed in classrooms at all levels and in all subject areas for students requiring more advanced work.

The purpose of this publication is to share ideas and strategies for practical implementation of the process. While geared primarily to teachers, it is also useful for principals and coordinators of gifted programs to read and implement.

Review of the Research

More has probably been written about the efficacy of accelerative practices with the gifted than about any other single educational intervention with any population. Reviews of the literature on acceleration have appeared with some regularity over the last 25 years (Benbow, 1991; Daurio, 1979; Gallagher, 1969; Gross & van Vliet, 2003; Kulik & Kulik, 1984; Reynolds, Birch, & Tuseth, 1962; VanTassel-Baska, 1986). Each review has carefully noted the overall positive impact of acceleration on gifted individuals at various stages in the lifespan. Successful programs of acceleration, most notably offshoots of the basic talent search model developed by Julian Stanley and others in the 1970s, have demonstrated the significant positive impact on the learning of students from using accelerative practices (Benbow & Stanley, 1983; Gross, 2004; Kulik & Kulik, 1992b; Swiatek & Benbow, 1991a, 1991b).

Moreover, a broad-based research agenda has emerged in the field of gifted education dedicated to understanding the long-term effects of educational acceleration of the gifted

(Brody, Assouline, & Stanley, 1990; Brody & Benbow, 1987; Brody & Stanley, 1991; Robinson & Janos, 1986; Swiatek & Benbow, 1991a, 1991b). These studies continue to show acceleration's positive results in cognitive development and a lack of negative effects on social/emotional development. Brody and Benbow reported no harmful effects of various forms of acceleration, including grade skipping and advanced course taking, among the Study of Mathematically Precocious Youth (SMPY) students subsequent to high school graduation. Accelerated students generally earned more overall honors and attended more prestigious colleges. Richardson and Benbow (1990) and Swiatek and Benbow (1991b) subsequently reported no harmful effects of acceleration on the social and emotional development or academic achievement after college graduation. Janos, Robinson, and Lunneborg (1989) also reported no detrimental effects of acceleration on young entrants to college. In another study, Robinson and Janos found similar adjustment patterns for early entrants in comparison to three equally able nonaccelerated comparison groups, noting only unconventionality as a distinguishing characteristic of the early entrants. Another study, this one of female-only early college entrants, found positive personality growth during the accelerated first year of the program (Cornell, Callahan, & Loyd, 1991). Finally, Brody et al. (1990) found that, among accelerated students, the best predictor of college achievement was early and continued Advanced Placement course taking, suggesting that advanced, challenging work on an ongoing basis is a powerful inducement to later achievement.

Such empirical support alone would lead one to expect that the world of educational practice would wholeheartedly embrace the concept of acceleration and find diverse ways to employ it effectively in many educational settings. Regrettably, this has not been the case. Instead, there has been a deliberate shunning of this approach by the educational establishment (Jones & Southern, 1992). Some insight was gained into the dynamics of this situation when the majority of gifted program coordinators themselves were found to be philosophically against the practice (Southern & Jones, 1991). A survey of program interventions used with the at-risk gifted (VanTassel-Baska, Patton, & Prillaman, 1991) also revealed that acceleration in some form finished fifth behind such approaches as independent study, college coursework, and various enrichment strategies. This relatively low status suggests that acceleration is not a routine strategy in gifted programs despite positive research evidence supporting its effectiveness.

One tool that has emerged in the past few years to help educators assess the need for acceleration practices is the Iowa Acceleration Scale (IAS) for Whole Grade Acceleration in grades K–8 (Assouline, Colangelo, Lupkowski-Shoplik, Lipscomb, & Forstadt, 2003). The IAS was modeled after the Light's Retention Scale and uses a numerical rating scale to provide structure for the acceleration decision process. The decision to accelerate a student can be controversial for both educators and parents. The scale therefore focuses on the child's intellectual and emotional development, as well as his or her maturity, attempting to address issues that could become problematic. This scale should be viewed as a tool to guide the discussion and decisions surrounding acceleration options available to gifted students. It is an attempt to take a completely subjective process and try to infuse an objective component into it. Earlier guidelines have also been delineated for considering the process of deciding on acceleration options (Feldhusen, Proctor, & Black, 1986; VanTassel-Baska, 1986).

Myths About Acceleration

Because acceleration options are used so infrequently, it is likely that many educators have not had direct experience with accelerated students or with various forms of acceleration. As a result, myths about the practice abound. The following list is typical in that it explores various misconceptions about acceleration that many educators and even parents hold.

Myth #1: Gifted children will become social and emotional misfits if they are accelerated. No studies suggest that acceleration causes such problems in the gifted (Gross, 1994; Gross & van Vliet, 2003; Kulik & Kulik, 1984). Ironically, just the opposite may be true: When forced to socialize with agemates in a lower level curriculum, gifted children may become socially withdrawn and alienated over time.

Myth #2: Gifted children benefit more when their learning is controlled, even when advancement is a part of the plan. For example, students may go ahead a half-year in math, but no more. This myth is dangerous in that it implies a one-size-fits-all mentality when working with the gifted. Individual differences prevail in ways that make artificial boundaries for learning a subject inhibitory. Each student should be encouraged to learn as much as possible in subject areas for which he or she must demonstrate proficiency (Heinbokel, 2002; Schiever & Maker, 1997).

Myth #3: Gifted children benefit from enrichment more than acceleration. Meta-analytic studies over the past century have continued to demonstrate that acceleration is twice as powerful as enrichment when dealing with gifted students (e.g., Kulik & Kulik, 1992a; Walberg & Reynolds, 1994). Moreover, gifted students enjoy moving at a fast pace through subject material, "gobbling up" new facts as they go. For many gifted students, their major interest area is also the area of learning in which they are the most precocious, thus adding to their desire for advanced work in that area.

Myth #4: Gifted children will run out of curriculum or have to repeat in later years because of early exposure to advanced level work. The new standards have clearly demonstrated the scope of material that needs to be mastered in each subject area, an amount requiring more instructional time than is currently available in schools (Marzano, 1999). Consequently, there will always be more to learn even for the gifted at every stage of development than could be formally taught. Schools need to be sensitive, however, to K–12 curricular planning for the gifted that would allow for effective use of school time in a subject area, augmented with outside opportunities (National Education Commission on Time and Learning, 1994).

Myth #5: Gifted children will be more normalized by staying with agemates. The reality of giftedness is its unique trajectory for learning that does not conform to age-grade expectations. Consequently, staying with agemates and being discouraged from learning at one's own comfortable rate invites underachievement patterns of behavior, including acting up and out, refusing to do assigned work, and loss of motivation for learning (Gallagher & Gallagher, 1994).

These are a few of the common myths held about the dangers of accelerating gifted learners. In truth, our gifted programs are far less effective than they might be if strong acceleration options were enacted, especially in respect to the curriculum.

The Perceived Effects of Acceleration

Individual perceptions about specific highly gifted students and their parents have also shaped our understandings of the purported dangers of accelerative practices. Such perceptions have also been fed by societal views of inappropriate parenting and aberrant development.

The Hurried Child

Elkind's (1981) book *The Hurried Child* described hazards that confront the child who is forced to grow up too soon and too fast. Unfortunately, the tide of his book has stuck in the public consciousness as a metaphor for a gifted child who moves more rapidly through education than age-level peers. Although Elkind did not address academic acceleration for gifted students, it is clear that he regards the lockstep, assembly line processing of children that is characteristic of American education as a major threat to the healthy development of young children. On this point, he shares the concerns that have led parents and educators to consider academic acceleration.

Elkind has since hedged on either accepting or rejecting the option, leaving the impression that he is ambivalent (e.g., Elkind, 1988). The image of the "hurried child" has, nevertheless, had a powerful effect on the development and rational evaluation of options for acceleration. The image conjures up the notion that the gifted child is being rushed through school—at the risk of his or her emotional well-being—in an effort to beat the clock before checking in as a bona fide "natural resource." Childhood is a precious time of innocence and discovery, and popular wisdom seems to ask, what's the rush? For example, to the casual observer, it seems that allowing capable children to take algebra at age 10 or at age 14 amounts to speeding up their education. Because this fast pace is considered a risk to the social/emotional development of the student, who will eventually take higher level courses anyway, it is sometimes difficult to justify the use of acceleration.

The validity of the "hurried child" metaphor is limited by the fallacy of two basic assumptions. First, it is assumed that the learner is actually hurried through school and childhood relationships. Second, it is also assumed that virtually all children who are capable of superior performances in advanced curricula will still be around and interested if they are forced to either wait for, or plod through, instruction along with their age-level peers. Neither assumption can be supported in fact. Thus, educators and parents who have squarely confronted the problems of meeting the needs of demonstrated precocity should not have to defend hurrying a child. More rapidly paced instruction and advanced placements can be legitimately regarded recognitions and accommodations of the abilities, achievements, and needs of capable learners.

The Maladaptive Child

Much debate has also arisen with respect to potential risks to the social and emotional development of students as a result of acceleration (e.g., Maddux, Stacy, & Scott, 1981; Obrzut,

Nelson, & Obrzut, 1984). Examples of poorly adjusted adults are "exhibited" as case studies of the ravages of acceleration over time (Daurio, 1979; Pressey, 1949). Some gifted children who have been accelerated will complain about problems such as being isolated in the classroom, being the last to drive, or feeling odd about being one of the last to go through puberty. Parents may perceive that their child is immature and, in hindsight, regret accelerating him or her. Although most gifted adolescents do not think that acceleration poses clear dangers, they are nevertheless skeptical about the effects it might have on their social relationships.

The effects of acceleration on social and emotional development have not been well researched. There exists a strong belief among educators and the general society that children's social and emotional adjustment is inextricably linked to associating with children born within 6 months of their own age for 13 years of schooling. Even though many studies have shown that factors such as family nurturance, the roles of significant others, and self-perception are more important in determining good social and emotional development than mere association with chronological age peers (VanTassel-Baska & Olszewski-Kubilius, 1988), there persists a specious argument that instructional placement with same-age peers will contribute substantially to reducing the development of maladaptive behavior among gifted students.

Acceleration Options

Precocious students, by definition, demonstrate accelerated development and learning compared with their same-age peers. What is provided in the name of acceleration are curricula and services that are appropriately paced and at an appropriate level to meet the needs of children who have demonstrated, compared with their peers, advanced learning and development. Numerous acceleration options are available for precocious children that can be tailored to the resources the school possesses, as well as the strengths of the individual child. The goal for schools is to develop a combination of acceleration options, enrichment options, and out-of-school opportunities that reflect appropriate education at a given point in time for a specific child. Acceleration options can be cost-effective and are practical, especially in rural areas where fewer students are available for gifted services.

Key acceleration options include the following:

- *Early admittance to school.* The student is allowed to enter school prior to the age specified by the district for entry into kindergarten. This is one of the best options for meeting the needs of gifted students whose advanced abilities are evident at an early age. It allows the student to enter school with a peer group with whom he or she will remain.

- *Grade skipping.* The student is allowed to move ahead of normal grade placement by one or more years. Grade skipping is especially recommended for highly gifted students who are advanced in all subjects relative to their classmates or for those gifted students who just missed the age cutoff for school entrance or were held back by their parents for a year because they were close to the age cutoff.

- *Entering college early with or without a high school diploma.* The student is allowed to leave school one year early in full standing to an advanced level of instruction at a local college or university. This option has become quite acceptable for highly gifted students in recent years.

- *Entering a college early-entrance program.* These programs are offered at special universities such as Simon's Rock College, the Texas Academy of Math and Science, Mary Baldwin College, and the University of Washington. Although they vary widely in their philosophy and approach, these programs are designed to meet the needs of students who are ready for college work, but would like to be part of a peer group who have made the same decision to leave high school early.

- *The International Baccalaureate (IB) program.* This program is designed to bring a common curriculum to multinational students living in countries throughout the world. The underlying philosophy of the program is to develop the whole student with challenging and in-depth learning experiences through a general and comprehensive curriculum at the precollegiate level that is pitched at a first-year university level.

- *Content acceleration.* Content acceleration involves taking a course 1 to 2 years earlier than is typical. If a student is reading at the level of the fourth graders in his or her school, but is placed chronologically in the second grade, the student should be allowed to take reading with the fourth graders.

- *Dual enrollment.* Students take advantage of college curricula at a local college, community college, or university while still enrolled in secondary school.

- *Taking special fast-paced classes during the summer or academic year.* This option allows middle school students to take high-school-level courses for credit or placement in 75 hours of instruction. College Board achievement tests in the subject are used to assess individual performances. There are many summer programs offering fast-paced courses across the United States. Some of the larger programs include Johns Hopkins University's Center for the Advancement of Academically Talent Youth (CTY), Duke University's Talent Identification Program, Northwestern University's Center for Talent Development, Purdue University's Gifted Education Resource Institute, Iowa State University's Office of Precollegiate Programs for Talented and Gifted, the University of Iowa, and the University of Denver's Rocky Mountain Talent Search.

- *Telescoping curricula.* The student spends less time than usual in a course of study (e.g., completes a 1-year course in a semester or completes 2 years of a subject in

1 year). The school may also provide for the student to finish 4 years of high school in 3 years. At the university level, students may earn both a bachelor's and master's degree in 4 years or a terminal degree in a 6-year program.

- *Compressing or compacting curricula.* Through this technique, the curriculum is compressed or compacted in such a way that gifted students can complete it in less time. One means of doing this is to allow students to skip those units in which they have already attained mastery and to streamline the follow-up content material.

- *Credit by examination.* The student receives credit at the high school or college level upon successful completion of an examination in a relevant subject.

- *Advanced Placement (AP) courses and examinations.* AP classes, which are different from honors courses, are college-level courses taught in high school that may garner college credit for the student if his or her final AP exam scores are sufficiently high.

- *Individual tutoring in advanced subject matter.* In some cases, school-based acceleration is not practical or advisable, and tutoring can be used to attend to the student's learning needs to ensure that he or she receives an education that is commensurate with his or her abilities.

- *Mentorships.* The student is exposed to a mentor who provides advanced training, experiences, and pacing in a content area.

The Relationship Between Acceleration and Enrichment

The fact that acceleration receives such little attention and acceptance among educators—including principals, school psychologists, and a fair proportion of coordinators of gifted education programs—speaks strongly to their rejection of the defining attributes of giftedness. Their rejection of acceleration also points to their lack of knowledge of the functional aspects of instructional options for gifted students. Enrichment activities are often preferred to acceleration by educators, parents, and students because they may have greater appeal on the grounds of novelty.

According to the usual distinction between acceleration and enrichment, acceleration gives precocious students the chance to proceed through the curriculum at a more rapid pace than age-level peers of more average aptitude, whereas enrichment provides elaborated instructional experiences, but not at a more rapid pace or a higher level. The logic of such a distinction between acceleration and enrichment is, however, indefensible. It ignores the fact that gifted students learn at a more rapid pace than do their agemates. By the time they appear as candidates for acceleration, they are already achieving at higher levels.

Enrichment activities seek to reduce emphasis on speed of learning in favor of emphasizing elaborated study. Through the use of enrichment techniques, students are kept at work on grade-level-appropriate tasks. Enrichment may concentrate on group problem solving and peer interaction, often including projects that are connected with social responsibility (e.g., environmental concerns or community service efforts). These activities are beneficial and appropriate for many students.

Yet, when they delay a student's academic progress or when their sole purpose is to maintain on-level placement, they are indefensible. To the extent that enrichment activities are devoid of advanced levels of instruction and study, they contribute to the general ambivalence about accommodating precocious students. Programs based solely on enrichment do not present sufficient challenge to highly able students. These students cannot be adequately served until schools are willing to accelerate the pace of instruction as needed by individuals and groups of gifted children.

Characteristics of Potential Accelerants

The question of who should participate in acceleration options cannot be easily generalized. The range of abilities, ages, and options are too broad for quick summary. It is, however, helpful to examine illustrative cases. Such descriptions illuminate important considerations regarding the process of acceleration. The following section will review several issues that are consistently important to the selection of successful candidates for acceleration.

Cognitive Ability and Performance

Students with superior intellectual abilities are able to manipulate abstract symbol systems much better than their average agemates. They are also able to learn complex new skills and process large amounts of information at faster rates. Many gifted students are early readers who are achieving 2 to 6 years above their age-level peers (Gallagher & Gallagher, 1994). Proceeding along in a lockstep instructional program with their peers is not appropriate for many highly capable learners. Acceleration could reasonably be considered if it appears that classroom instruction is characterized by

1. a dearth of new skills and knowledge being presented,

2. incremental progression through a repetitive series of developmental skills exercises, and

3. the precocious student's rapidly gaining the given objective and then being required or allowed to mill about until the rest of the class catches up.

Such situations become extremely problematic for capable learners. If students who learn at an exceptionally rapid pace are required to slow down and wait for peers to catch up, they will almost certainly fail to come close to their potential for academic achievement.

Students in the upper 2% of the general population of measured intelligence have been considered good candidates for acceleration. For an acceleration of 2 years, Gallagher and Gallagher (1994) advocated that students have IQs of 130 or above. Terman and Oden (1947) chose an IQ cutoff of 135 to recommend 2 or more years' acceleration. In addition to general measures of intellect, performance on specific achievement and aptitude tests are frequently used to make decisions about particular subject-matter acceleration (Benbow & Stanley, 1983). Subject-matter acceleration would be advisable for students whose exceptional achievements are limited to certain areas and are so pronounced that they would need instruction at a significantly higher level than is provided to their agemates.

Affective Characteristics

Many gifted learners will exhibit boredom and impatience if they are forced to be schooled at the level of their same-aged peers (Clark, 2002). The disparity between the pacing of instruction and their demonstrated abilities to learn can contribute to inattention, boredom, frustration, and inappropriate social and emotional behavior in highly capable learners. Concern is frequently expressed over the possibility that students will experience difficulties if they are separated from their same-age peers or schooled with older classmates. However, concern is also in order if they lack interaction with intellectual peers. The only satisfactory situation for the gifted child who has been neglected in the regular classroom is to find "learning mates." Such peers may be obtained through the formation of advanced instructional programs or through placement in grades or classes one or more levels ahead of the student's current placement.

Interest and Motivation to Be Accelerated

The interest of a student in participating in different acceleration options is a crucial variable for consideration. Students must want to be accelerated. They must understand the needs and implications of acceleration regardless of the type employed. Not all students who are able to handle accelerated programs may wish to participate in them.

Students should be consulted about such program opportunities, with a competent adult explaining the relative advantages of the programs. Potential drawbacks should also be noted. For example, it may mean leaving friends who are agemates in a given classroom, doing more work, and being presented with a greater challenge. For some students, acceleration would not be an acceptable option. As long as the case is made, it seems prudent to allow students to decide for themselves.

Success in accelerative programs depends on the student's motivation and commitment to succeed, as well as his or her ability. Parents and educators must, however, encourage gifted learners to participate in challenging learning situations that may include accelerative aspects, such as classes at museums or planetariums, summer courses at universities, special interest clubs for adults in computers or rocketry, and dozens of similar opportunities. On the other hand, it should not be an option for gifted students to avoid difficult or challenging work. The lack of appropriate levels of instruction and expectations for performance may bring about intellectual laziness in gifted students—a problem that may be very difficult to overcome.

Curricular Emphases for Accelerated Study in Reading and Math

A basic principle of instruction for gifted education is that many gifted learners need content acceleration at a number of stages in their development (VanTassel-Baska & Little, 2003). Although a district's programs may include elaborations on basic materials and activities that enrich, expand, and enhance learning opportunities, it must be recognized that a student's aptitude for accelerated learning is fundamental to the operation of the program and its benefits. It may be difficult to obtain a program that is consistently fast-paced, enriching, and well organized. Yet, such goals must be targeted if the student's needs are to be met, particularly in the subjects of reading and mathematics. While other subject areas would also require accelerated study, the areas of reading and mathematics as tool skills begun and emphasized strongly in the K–5 curriculum in all school districts suggests that these areas need special attention.

As an example, in a program for primary-grade students reading at advanced levels, the following program components would be appropriate. District personnel may use the following list as a self-assessment on existing options for acceleration in the language arts:

- work from a program for advanced grade levels;
- participate in an inquiry-based study of appropriate classical and contemporary literature;
- engage in a writing program that encourages elaboration and incorporation of ideas from literature into stories;
- use supplementary materials for the development of vocabulary skills;
- read selected biographies and books in the content areas (including subjects dealing with multicultural issues);
- have learning experiences in a foreign language of choice;
- use logic and critical thinking;
- learn spelling from both basal and literary reading selections;
- tell stories and read one's own stories; and
- pursue free reading based on individual interests.

Although the overall emphasis of the program is whole-language experiences with a strong emphasis on enrichment of the basic curriculum, the underlying issue of appropriate level of instruction is stressed through careful assessment of reading-skill levels at various stages during the year, access to advanced reading materials (including basal and literature programs), and a vocabulary and spelling program that corresponds to the level of reading instruction. This list of interventions for gifted learners at the primary school shows the scope of activities that acceleration should provide in setting the curricular pattern in every content area.

Subject-matter acceleration in another content area also has clear importance for students in the primary grades. In mathematics, for example, there is the need to consider the following emphases beyond the preassessment. Again, districts may use the following list for self-assessment purposes:

- develop spatial skills and concepts through geometry and other media;
- use problem-solving skills with appropriately challenging problems;
- use calculators and computers as tools in the problem-solving process;
- engage in learning mathematical concepts deeply and well;
- focus on logic problems that require deductive thinking skills and inference;
- apply mathematics in the real world through special projects;
- work on algebraic manipulations; and
- work with statistics and probability.

Again, the accelerated mathematics curriculum is balanced with a strong enrichment element; but, at the same time, it allows for skills, concepts, and requisite materials to be at a challenging level for the child, rather than gearing everything to grade-level considerations.

Strategies for Acceleration in Classrooms

The following set of four classroom strategies outline important modifications that can be made by teachers to ensure effective education of the gifted through the use of an accelerative mode of instruction.

Strategy 1: Selecting Differentiated Curricular Materials

The first strategy suggested for classroom adaptation of acceleration is the selection of materials already representative of advanced-level content and other differentiation features. These materials have proven to be effective with gifted learners and suggest that real learning occurs when they are artfully employed by teachers (VanTassel-Baska, 2003). A sample list of such materials is provided with a form for selection (see Figures 1 and 2). The idea of teachers selecting materials, rather than creating them, speaks to the limited time teachers have available to engage in direct curriculum development work. Many times, it is simply not feasible; thus, existing curricular materials become an attractive alternative. In order to employ this strategy, a three-step process is necessary.

Step 1. Teachers should compile a list of potential materials for review by content area and grade levels (see Figure 1). A school librarian should be helpful in this task. The list provided in Figure 2 is also a good starting place because it contains materials that meet the appropriate standards for use with gifted learners.

Step 2. Once the materials are available and are ready for review, teachers may complete the criteria checklist provided in Figure 1 to assess the appropriateness of the material for the concepts and standards to be addressed.

Step 3. Teachers implement the text material selected as suggested and engage in appropriate pre- and posttesting.

Strategy 2: Diagnostic–Prescriptive Instruction

For the clear majority of gifted and high-ability learners in school, the use of classroom-based acceleration practices are an essential part of making learning meaningful for them. A system for diagnosing and prescribing the appropriate level of instruction for these learners was developed in the 1970s by Julian Stanley and has been used worldwide in programs for the gifted ever since (Benbow & Stanley, 1983; VanTassel-Baska, 1996). The core of this diagnostic–prescriptive approach may be summarized in three steps: diagnostic assessment, cluster grouping, and follow-up curricular intervention.

Step 1: Diagnostic Assessment. Perhaps the central strategy that is called for is effective diagnostic assessment of those learners the teacher suspects of having advanced abilities in the core areas of learning: reading and math. This diagnostic assessment should be buttressed by the previous year's achievement

1. Course and subject area: ______________________________

2. Grade level: ______________________________

3. Collect relevant materials from publishers and your librarian, asking that materials*:

    1. be two grade levels above the reading level of typical students at the grade level to be taught;
    2. have evidence of use with students two grade levels above placement in selected districts;
    3. have evidence of effectiveness with gifted learners.

4. These materials then should be reviewed, using the following checklist:

Yes	No	
___	___	selected activities, resources, and materials are sufficiently challenging for advanced learners
___	___	organizing concept is treated in sufficient depth
___	___	opportunities are provided for creative production
___	___	opportunities are provided for integrating higher order thought processes
___	___	issues, problems, and themes are sufficiently complex
___	___	ample opportunities are provided through unit activities for students to construct meaning for themselves
___	___	both content and instruction provide for a sufficiently high level of abstraction
___	___	reading material is sufficiently advanced
___	___	different levels of ability are provided in the unit
___	___	open-ended questions that encourage multiple or divergent responses are identified for the teacher
___	___	opportunities are provided for independent learning
___	___	opportunities are provided for meaningful project work

Figure 1. Selecting Differentiated Materials Form

Note. Adapted from *Content-Based Curriculum for Gifted Learners* (pp. 269–270), ed. by J. VanTassel-Baska & C. Little, 2003, Waco, TX: Prufrock Press. Copyright ©2003 The Center for Gifted Education. Adapted with permission.

* Packaged materials that already meet these criteria appear in Figure 2.

Subject	K–3	4–6	7–8	9–12
Math	• Everyday Math • TIMS (Teaching Integrated Math and Science) • TOPS (Techniques of Problem Solving) • NCTM Navigations Series	• Everyday Math • TIMS (Teaching Integrated Math and Science) • TOPS (Techniques of Problem Solving) • NCTM Navigations Series • Connected Math	• Math the Human Endeavor • TIMS (Teaching Integrated Math and Science) • TOPS (Techniques of Problem Solving) • NCTM Navigations Series	• Discovering Geometry: An Inductive Approach • TOPS (Techniques of Problem Solving) • NCTM Navigations Series • Twists and Turns and Tangles in Math and Physics • AP Syllabi in Calculus and Probability & Statistics
Social Studies	• College of William and Mary Social Studies Units • Touchpebbles	• College of William and Mary Social Studies Units • MACOS (Man a Course of Study) • Voyage of the Mimi	• College of William and Mary Social Studies Units • Contemporary Perspectives (Greenhaven Press)	• College of William and Mary Social Studies Units • PBLISS (Problem Based Learning in Social Studies) by S. Gallagher • Contemporary Perspectives (Greenhaven Press) • AP Syllabi in American History, Psychology, Economics, European History

Language Arts	• College of William and Mary Language Arts Units • College of William and Mary Navigator Novel Study Guides • Jr. Great Books	• College of William and Mary Language Arts Units • College of William and Mary Navigator Novel Study Guides • Philosophy for Children • Jr. Great Books	• College of William and Mary Language Arts Units • College of William and Mary Navigator Novel Study Guides • Jr. Great Books	• College of William and Mary Language Arts Units • College of William and Mary Navigator Novel Study Guides • Conversations: Readings for Writing • AP/IB Syllabi
Science	• College of William and Mary PBL Science Units • FOSS (Full Option Science System) • GEMS (Great Explorations in Math and Science) • Insights: A Hands-on Elementary Science Curriculum • Science for Life and Living		• College of William and Mary PBL Science Units • FAST (Foundational Approaches in Science Teaching) • Middle School Life Science	• Biological Sciences Curriculum Study (BSCS) • Modeling Instruction in High School Physics • AP/IB Syllabi

Figure 2. Materials That Meet the Appropriate Standards for Use With Gifted Learners

Note. See Resources for complete references for these materials.

data and other records. Utilizing multiple sources of data for making decisions is important. Possible sources of diagnostic data include the following:

- *End-of-year assessments to be employed at current grade level.* In September, give your students the end-of-year reading comprehension, spelling, and English usage tests in language arts; in math, give them the end-of-year computation, measurement, and number theory assessments. In each of these areas, high-ability learners are likely to score 85% or higher, necessitating the need for compressed instruction and advanced work on other aspects of the language arts and math curricula.

- *Formal diagnostic instruments.* Give students the Gates-McGinitie diagnostic reading test, the Orleans-Hanna math test, or both to assess functional level in these skill areas. Teachers may also administer an individual achievement test in these key areas of learning.

- *Chapter tests that cluster items across topics in math.* Because of the incremental nature of math study, it is advised that students be assessed on more discrete aspects of the curriculum as the year progresses. While this approach inhibits overall accelerative practices, it does allow students to avoid being remediated.

Such diagnostic assessment is a crucial first step in finding students who need advanced instruction in basic areas of the curriculum.

Step 2: Cluster Grouping. Follow-up instructional intervention must then be based on the diagnostic results. These results should be analyzed for patterns within and across student profiles. Students who are reasonably close in scores (i.e., within 10 percentile points) should be cluster-grouped for advanced instruction. These groups may range from two to five students in number. If the teacher has only one student who is very advanced, that student should be cluster-grouped with other students at a comparable level, either at the same grade level or at the next grade level for instruction in reading, math, or both. It is not appropriate to have gifted students working independently throughout the year in a core area of the curriculum when they could be working with intellectual peers and learning more.

Step 3: Intervention With Curricular Materials. Beyond the instructional grouping decision lies the issue of a differentiated instructional plan for these students, especially in reading and mathematics during the elementary years. The combinatory power of diagnostic testing, cluster grouping based on results, and follow-up intervention would be a major improvement in all classrooms and would ease the concerns of parents of the gifted whose children feel trapped by grade-level work.

Figure 3 and 4 present forms that provide a basis for teachers to use this strategy and record its process and progress for the learner. If a student tests out entirely, an additional form (see Figure 5) is provided to document important data related to that decision, as well.

Figure 6 presents a case example of a student's individual learning plan depicting the use of the diagnostic–prescriptive strategy in mathematics. It also depicts curricular decisions to (1) differentiate math materials, (2) test out of fourth-grade math, (3) provide strong content instruction in math, and (4) use creative projects to ensure curricular variety. Assessment of the student is also recommended at appropriate intervals throughout the year.

The Prescriber Monitor, developed by the Muskingum Valley Educational Service Center (ESC), is a teaching tool for using the diagnostic–prescriptive approach routinely in assessing gifted student progress through the mathematics standards in Ohio. The sample provided in Figure 7 shows the form for

1. Student ______________________________

2. Course subject/Content area ______________________________

3. Diagnostic (pre)assessment test employed that covers the year's content to be taught: ______________________________

4. Percentage mastered for each major concept/standard tested:

   Concept/Standard % Mastered

5. Using a criterion of 85% mastery, what areas of the curriculum can be eliminated from teaching for this student? (List standards and textbook chapters.) If the student has achieved 85% mastery in all concepts/standards, please complete the attached "testing out" form.

6. Given a mastery level of 50%, what areas of the curriculum can be handled more rapidly and more superficially?

7. Given these mastery levels in the curriculum, what concepts need to be taught fully, but at a rate commensurate with the student's capacity?

continued on next page

8. On a separate page, display a reorganized prescription for a year's work, showing the state objectives linked to concepts to be taught, with sample references to text pages and other materials.

9. Comment below on the student's perceived strengths and weaknesses in the subject areas based on your analysis of diagnostic test data:

Strengths	Weaknesses

10. Posttest the student at relevant junctures during the year, coinciding with regular classroom assessments as much as possible. Construct more complex performance-based assessments on the material as appropriate based on the student's assignment and learning cycle.

Figure 3. Diagnostic–Prescriptive Curriculum Analysis Form

Note. This form is to be completed in September based on a year or semester in a course/content area.

sixth grade and selected National Council of Teachers of Mathematics standards addressing Strand "a" on the Number, Number Sense, and Operations Standard.

Strategy 3: Reorganizing the Curriculum

Another classroom strategy that allows students to accelerate appropriately is a reorganization or compression of content around higher order skills and concepts. This approach has been used effectively in teaching Latin (VanTassel-Baska, 2004), mathematics, and science. It calls for teachers to have strong content knowledge and understand the standards in their relevant area of study. This strategy may also be broken down into specific stages:

1. Student `Sally Sloan`

2. Course subject/Content area `5th grade`

3. Diagnostic (pre)assessment test employed that covers the year's content to be taught: `End of math book`

4. Percentage mastered for each major concept/standard tested:

Concept/Standard	% Mastered
Spatial reasoning	80%
Measurement	100%
Computation	92%
Logic	95%
Statistics	75%
Number theory	85%
Problem solving	95%

5. Using a criterion of 85% mastery, what areas of the curriculum can be eliminated from teaching for this student? (List standards and textbook chapters.) If the student has achieved 85% mastery in all concepts/standards, please complete the attached "testing out" form.

   Measurement (testing covers relevant standards)
   Computation (testing covers relevant standards)
   Logic (testing covers relevant standards)
   Number theory (testing covers relevant standards)
   Problem solving (testing covers relevant standards)

6. Given a mastery level of 50%, what areas of the curriculum can be handled more rapidly and more superficially?

   Spatial reasoning
   Statistics

7. Given these mastery levels in the curriculum, what concepts need to be taught fully, but at a rate commensurate with the student's capacity?

   None

continued on next page

8. On a separate page, display a reorganized prescription for a year's work, showing the state objectives linked to concepts to be taught, with sample references to text pages and other materials.

9. Comment below on the student's perceived strengths and weaknesses in the subject areas based on your analysis of diagnostic test data:

Strengths	Weaknesses
Basic math facts, principles, and computation skills Facility with higher order math skills such as problem solving and logic	None apparent (Areas below 85% are only relatively weaker, but very strong for a pre-test score.)

10. Posttest the student at relevant junctures during the year, coinciding with regular classroom assessments as much as possible. Construct more complex performance-based assessments on the material as appropriate based on the student's assignment and learning cycle.

Figure 4. Completed Diagnostic–Prescriptive Curriculum Analysis Form

Note. This form is to be completed in September based on a year or semester in a course/content area.

Stage 1. Teachers need to review their text materials and outline the scope and sequence of topics to be taught. They need to think through each topic in respect to state standard segments and fill in missing topics. Once this task has been completed, teachers may wish to consider ways to combine topics, synthesize them, or reduce or amplify particular emphases based on knowing the characteristics of gifted children for quick recall and logical thinking.

Stage 2. Teachers now may wish to consider the list of higher order concepts and skills employed frequently in gifted programs. Selecting one concept and three skills to use as reorganiz-

1. Student ____

2. Course/Subject ____

3. Grade level and year in subject: ____________________________

4. Reasons for allowing student to test out:

5. Recommendation of last year's teacher regarding the relevant area of learning:

6. Test administered:____

   Date: ______________ Overall score*: ______________________

   Subscores: ____

* 85% mastery in all areas may be viewed as a typical criterion level for testing out.

7. Check one of the following:

____ Student performed at appropriate criterion level on the test to receive advanced placement (and credit, if appropriate or needed).

____ Student failed to perform at appropriate criterion level on the test. No credit or advanced placement will be given at this time.

8. Placement decision based on student performance on the test:

9. Assigned curriculum follow-up to testing:

Figure 5. Testing Out of Curriculum Form

Student Name: Barry Jones   Date: September, 2004
Grade: 4   Teacher: Mrs. Smith

Assessment Information
Achievement: Reading: 99.9   Math: 99.9   IQ: 133
Other:

Personal Interests: sports (statistics of players), brainteasers, architect studies, music

Needs to Address	Differentiated Strategies/Interventions	Person(s) Responsible	Evaluation
MATH • Pretested out of all of Saxon Math 4th grade • Attends 4th-grade gifted math • Currently working in 5th-grade Saxon series (almost completed) • Completed specific units in Investigations 4th and 5th grade	• Excuse Barry from Saxon math materials based on documentation of Saxon math units completed through 5th grade. Replace with Connected Math 6th grade with teacher of gifted providing the curriculum on a daily basis (including weight grading as determined by the regular classroom teacher and teacher of gifted).	Mrs. Smith 4th-Grade Teacher	Records of completed and graded activities and projects in Connected Math 4th-grade proficiency tests results Midyear individual testing—print results for age peers and grade peers
	• Attend 5th grade gifted math once per week for peer relationships	4th-Grade Teacher	
	• Use some math time for creative projects, especially in music, sports, and sciences (Resource room program) • Give Barry the practice test for review and the final test as part of his math grade on the report card. • Reassess Barry mid-4th-grade year to measure math levels.	Coordinator of Gifted	

Figure 6. Individual Learning Plan

Students	a.6.1 Decompose and recompose whole numbers using factors and exponents, and explain why "squared" means "second power" and "cubed" means "third power."	a.6.2 Find and use the prime factorization of composite numbers. For example: a) use the prime factorization to recognize the greatest common factor (GCF).	a.6.3 Explain why a number is referred to as being "rational," and recognize that the expression *a*/*b* can mean a parts of size 1/*b* each, *a* divided by *b* or the ratio of *a* to *b*.	a.6.4 Describe what it means to find a specific percent of a number using real-life examples.
	Correlates with (NS) Benchmark G	Correlates with (NS) Benchmark G	Correlates with (NS) Benchmark G	Correlates with (NS) Benchmark G
1 Barry	1	1	1	1
2 Sally	1	1	2	2
3 Charles	1	1	3	3
4 Melody	1	1	2	3

Figure 7. Sample Form: The Prescriber: Indicator Monitoring Record Mathematics 6th Grade

Note. 1 = Mastered, 2 = Developing, 3 = Needs focused instruction

ers may be enough to tackle at one time. Or, teachers may merely want to use specific content-based concepts for reorganizing topics. In science, for example, the concepts of change and systems fit well with teaching the science standards in many states.

Stage 3. Teachers now need to develop activities and questions to guide student learning in the reorganized content area. Use of scaffolds for learning may be helpful at this level, including the sample concept maps provided in Figure 8.

Strategy 4: Curriculum Compacting

A third strategy for teachers to accelerate learning for gifted students is through the compacting process. If the teacher desires to compact instruction in only one area and do so in a piecemeal fashion (chapter topic by chapter topic), then curriculum compacting may be the answer. The purpose of compacting is also different in that it is used most frequently to remove gifted students from studying the given content area and place them instead in teacher-student mutually agreed upon project work. Such a shift in emphasis necessitates a careful calibration of compacted material. Again, a set of steps may be followed to accomplish curriculum compacting (Renzulli, Smith, & Reis, 1982):

Step 1. Teachers need to examine their content standards for potential topics that might be compacted for a few advanced students. Areas for easy compacting might be computational procedures in mathematics, grammar and usage in English, and science principles.

Step 2. Teachers may now make decisions about the pretest and posttest to be employed. Many teachers use review tests for the preassessment and the chapter test for the postassessment. Teachers may also construct their own test or use others that are both applicable to the topic and available.

1. Student ____

2. Course/Subject/Content area ___________________________

3. Provide a complete outline of topics to be taught in the course for the year or attach a content outline from the text to be employed:

4. Analyze the following list of concepts and select a few concepts as a basis for reorganization of your course/subject.

Top 12 Higher Order Concepts	
change	interdependence
systems	cause and effect
scale	models
reductionism	evolution
patterns	tolerance
structures	diversity

5. Analyze the following list of higher order skills and select a few skills as a basis for reorganization of your course/subject.

Top 12 Higher Order Skills	
analysis	drawing implications
interpretation	stating purpose
synthesis	identifying assumptions
creation	articulating multiple perspectives
evaluation	developing arguments
inferencing	problem finding and solving

6. Reorganize topics under the relevant concepts and skills listed:

Concept(s) ________________ Skills: ______________________

Relevant Topics: Applied skills:

continued on next page

7. Learn about the concept(s) selected and apply them to your subject by creating relevant generalizations and showing the applications to your course content.

8. Learn about the higher order skills selected and apply them to your course content by framing relevant activities and questions.

9. Use appropriate concept mapping techniques to teach students how higher order skills and concepts connect to lower order ones.

   Example of concept:

   Example of higher order skills:

Figure 8. Curriculum Reorganization Form

Step 3. Teachers need to administer the pretest and score it for levels of performance. Students who perform well (at or above 85%) on the preassessment may compact out of the curriculum content topic and be assigned advanced work in some form. For students at different levels of mastery, teachers can now streamline the teaching for them, covering only the material they do not know at a more rapid pace.

Step 4. For targeted students who have compacted out,

teachers may provide a set of options that could include (1) accelerating to the next topic in the core curricular area or (2) selecting a special project of interest to complete while the topic is being treated in class.

Step 5. After completing one of the options provided, students may now take the posttest with the rest of the class, bringing to an end one compacting episode. Teachers will need to document the level of performance on the posttest and assess the relevant alternative option as well (e.g., project or advanced study on another content topic).

Step 6. A new cycle of compacting using another topic may begin.

1. Student ______________________________

2. Course/Subject ______________________________

3. Name of pretest and chapter or unit to be compacted (identify test and content topics) ______________________________

4. Indicate percent of mastery of chapter or unit material tested by topic:
   Topic % of Mastery

5. Using a predetermined criterion level (usually 85%), determine what content may be eliminated from teaching for this student. (Cite topics here)

6. Using a predetermined criterion level (usually 50%), determine what topics may be taught more rapidly and cursorily? (Cite topics here.)

7. Based on chapter/unit preassessment results, what topics require full teaching? (Adjust the rate of teaching to the student's rate of learning.)

8. Estimate the amount of time to be saved through compacting and work with the student to plan a special project of interest during the time frame determined.

9. Posttest the student on the chapter/unit at the same time as other students to assure on-going mastery; assess the student's alternative learning option.

10. Plan to repeat the pretesting process for each relevant unit.

Figure 9: Curriculum Compacting Form

Note. This form is to be completed at appropriate times during the year.

An Acceleration Case Study

In order to assess the connection among acceleration theory, research, and practical ideas, it may be necessary to think through the ideas presented thus far in relationship to a real gifted child. The hypothetical John has been selected as a model because his age, his uneven profile of functional development, and his gender may impact our thinking about accelerative options.

John is a 6-year-old boy who shows extraordinary ability and interest in mathematics, topping out on in-grade achievement measures and scoring at the level of fifth graders on the Peabody Individual Achievement Test (PIAT) in the Math Concepts section. His father, an engineer, and his mother, a teacher, support his mathematical interest. John enjoys doing math at home on Saturdays, and he also enjoys "playing around" with mechanical objects in his spare time. His reading abilities are at the level of a second grader, and his record in other first-grade subjects is excellent. His kindergarten and first-grade teachers perceive John to be very able, and each has commented on her inability to challenge him sufficiently in mathematics. John, however, is small for his age and has displayed inappropriate social behavior in the classroom. His organizational skills are not remarkable, and he is frequently inattentive.

The following data suggest that some accelerative option would be appropriate:

1. John is highly advanced in one academic area (mathematics).

2. John's other academic performance is above average.

3. John's interests are in the direction of his apparent strengths.

4. John's parents are supportive of his learning, particularly in mathematics.

On the other hand, some factors suggest that some acceleration options may not be appropriate.

1. John has not managed to develop socially appropriate responses to the classroom demands for compliance and self-discipline.

2. Although he is a good student, John's precocity in mathematics is not evenly matched by his performance in other academic areas.

3. John is only 6 years old. He has only just begun first grade, so his adjustment to the school routines and demands is only beginning to develop.

4. John is small for his age.

After an examination of the evidence both for and against accelerating John, it may be useful to raise related issues concerning his candidacy for acceleration. As reasonable questions, one could pose the following:

1. *Which acceleration options would be most profitable for John?*

   Although a case could be made for grade skipping, the evidence clearly indicates that acceleration in mathematics is a more appropriate option.

2. *Does it appear likely that John would progress rapidly in all academic areas if given a program that would allow such opportunities?*

   Perhaps a telescoped option is preferable. John would be able to move through second- and third-grade curricular skills in all areas based on his readiness to do so.

3. *What should be reasonable expectations for performance and achievement?*

   If acceleration is limited to instruction in mathematics, then a more radical departure from the performances of age-level peers would be a reasonable expectation. On the other hand, if the instructional program provides for accelerated learning in all academic areas, then perhaps more modest goals should be expected.

Given the facts of this case, it is justifiable to provide some form of acceleration for John, and it would be unconscionable to ignore his abilities and achievements. Definitely, content acceleration in mathematics is required through one of the techniques described in this book. A diagnostic–prescriptive approach should be tried first, with possible testing out at relevant stages of development. The use of well-designed and advanced mathematics materials would also be appropriate. Finally, working with a content expert in math might lead to a reorganization of mathematics material to make it more efficient and gratifying for John. Thus, three of the strategies suggested might be implemented together over time to meet John's ongoing needs for advanced mathematics.

Organizational Necessities to Meet Gifted Students' Needs

An important problem in accommodating the needs of gifted students like John becomes apparent: The current organizational structure of our schools does not provide sufficient flexibility to readily allow a broad range of options to accommodate the various needs of such potential accelerants. Schools clearly need to consider the following types of curricular flexibility:

- younger students placed in advanced-level courses, including early entrance, grade skipping, telescoping, and subject-matter acceleration;
- credit, placement, or both for achievement completed outside the school program;
- substitutions for required courses;
- college credit and high school credit earned simultaneously;

- flexible time for demonstrating subject-matter proficiency; and
- opportunities to explore specific topics of interest.

If such curricular flexibility were prevalent in schools, addressing the needs of the gifted might become everyday practice across the country.

Figure 10 indicates some features of various typical candidates for acceleration and suggests reasonable paths of academic development. Ideally, the practice of acceleration is the act of providing optimal learning situations with an appropriately matched curriculum. The setting in which the acceleration is facilitated should be a secondary consideration. Excellent classroom teachers can accommodate such needs in their own classrooms with individualized educational planning. If the teacher lacks the skills, resources, or confidence to address the gifted child's need for accelerated learning, an advanced placement or a separate class grouping may be in order.

Early Admission

Students who are developmentally advanced in all academic areas by at least 2 years; identified by parents and confirmed by a psychologist.

Suggested Intervention: Early entrance to kindergarten with appropriately advanced curriculum, careful monitoring of progress throughout early elementary years. Additional acceleration will probably be warranted by junior high school. Early graduation from high school may also be considered (Proctor, Black, & Feldhusen, 1986).

Content Acceleration

Students who exhibit precocity in verbal areas, mathematical areas, or both; above average in other academic endeavors; identified by teachers during the primary years of schooling.

Suggested Intervention: Content acceleration to appropriately challenging levels in reading, math, or both; early application of abilities to writing, dramatics, and debate in the verbal area and to logic, spatial reasoning, and statistics in the math area (VanTassel-Baska & Little, 2003).

Grade Advancement

Students who are developmentally advanced in all academic areas with above-average (but not outstanding) grades; require different services than those offered in the regular classroom; identified by parents/self through talent search participation at junior high level.

Suggested Intervention: Grade acceleration to high school; course selection and program guided by academic strengths and interests; careful monitoring of performance in advanced classes to ensure both challenge and success (Stanley, 1979).

Early Exit From High School

Students who are highly motivated and excel in all areas at the high school level; identified by teachers as possible recipients for awards.

Suggested Intervention: Early graduation from high school with emphasis on career counseling for college selection of appropriate course of study (Stanley, 1979).

Figure 10. Archetypal Features of Candidates for Acceleration Matched With Intervention

Who Can Work With Accelerated Learners?

Good teachers can accommodate the placement of a precocious child in their classes. If, however, an instructional option is seriously intended to provide an opportunity to accelerate a capable child's learning, it will take an exceptional teacher. Following are several ideal qualities that should be sought in teachers of accelerated students:

1. *Eager backing of acceleration options for able learners.* The attitude of the teacher toward acceleration will have a critical influence on the adaptation and progress of accelerated students. Whereas accelerants are likely to have difficulties in classrooms where resistant teachers attribute most problems to their young age, neither can it be expected that they will fare well in classrooms where their advanced placements are merely tolerated. A teacher should be able to rise to the challenge of accelerating the learning of capable students. Such a teacher will furnish educational activities, plan and fol-

low strategies, and set expectations that will promote and maintain accelerated achievement. Teachers need to carry out frequent assessments of the accelerant's achievement and adjustment. If difficulties appear, they should be analyzed and dealt with promptly and rationally.

2. *Capability to adapt and modify a curriculum to provide accelerative experiences.* Teachers chosen to work with these students need to understand how to compress material, select key concepts for emphasis, and share knowledge systems with their students. They should not double the homework amount or cover more material in class (VanTassel-Baska & Olszewski-Kubilius, 1988).

3. *Adequate training and competence for teaching in the content area of the program.* Capable learners should have teachers who are eminently prepared to teach subject matter. This is especially true of accelerated learners. Their exceptional aptitudes will allow them to acquire new skills and knowledge rapidly and to explore issues that students in the regular class programs will not have time to address. Teachers need to prepare for incorporating appropriate content expertise, arranging mentorships, and setting up alternative learning placements, such as laboratories, clinics, and internships (VanTassel-Baska & Olszewski-Kubilius, 1988).

4. *Preparation in organizing and managing classroom activities.* A teacher of an accelerated program of study must be extremely conscious of the differences within any accelerated group of learners. Some will be capable of moving very rapidly, while others may wish to explore an area of interest in greater depth. Classroom environments should be flexible enough to accommodate such individual differences. Skill in the use of cluster group-

ing and regrouping within an accelerated program is highly desirable for such teachers. Teachers of accelerated students can use student contracts, academic centers in the classroom, independent reading time, and library-based study to assure integration of the range of student needs.

Making Acceleration a Useful Option

School districts will need to plan and prepare carefully to ensure that accelerative experiences will have beneficial effects for students. Networks of content area experts, artists, and educators from all levels and sectors of the community should be created, developed, and used to discuss acceleration issues, produce cooperative plans, and identify other mentors and resource people. Preschool educators and university experts in early childhood should be involved from the beginning because early referral is an important aspect of any acceleration plan. A task force network should, for example, address the need to devise appropriate curricula and to examine logistical issues regarding early entrance and early exit options.

In order to maximize curricular and program flexibility, it may be appropriate to develop written policy statements regarding acceleration. Indefensible restrictions should be removed to ensure that capable students will have maximum opportunities in the educational system—not be merely confined in it. Minimally, provisions need to be considered for the following opportunities:

1. continuous progress based on ability and performance, not age or grade, in individual curriculum areas;

2. early entrance to school;

3. appropriate credit, placement, or both for advanced coursework taken off campus, given validation of proficiency; and

4. early involvement in college work through the College Board Advanced Placement program or local arrangements with institutions of higher education for dual enrollment.

Responsible School Decision Making: Policy Recommendations

Educating our most able learners in appropriate ways is a challenge that this society must take seriously. Schools can ill afford to foster underachievement, disaffection, and alienation among gifted students. Even now, international comparisons on achievement, dropout rates, and delinquency data suggest that a disproportionately high percentage of our most capable learners are not maximizing their abilities.

The following list of policy recommendations is made in the hope that policies and procedures on acceleration might be adopted by local boards of education sensitive to the nature and needs of the gifted in their communities.

Acceleration Policies for the Gifted Learner

1. Each learner is entitled to experience learning at a level of challenge defined as task difficulty level slightly above skill mastery. For gifted learners, this implies the

opportunity for continuous progress through the basic curriculum based on demonstrated mastery of prior material. In all planned curricular experiences for the gifted, care must be taken to ensure that students are placed at their instructional level. This level may be determined by diagnostic testing, observation of mastery, or performance-based assessments.

2. Gifted learners should be afforded the opportunity to begin school-based experiences based on readiness and to exit them based on proficiency. Thus, both early entrance and early exit options should be provided. The gifted learner requires a school system to be flexible about when and where learning takes place. Optimally, some students can be best served by a pre-reading program at age 4; other students may be well served by college opportunities at age 16. Individual variables must be honored in an overall flexible system of implementation.

3. Some gifted learners may profit from telescoping 2 years of education into 1 or by bypassing a particular grade level. Provision for such advanced placement should be made based on individual student demonstration of capacity, readiness, and motivation. Placement in actual grade levels should be determined by many factors beyond age. Tailoring learning levels, as well as bypassing them, is another important way to ensure implementation of this policy.

Conclusion

Acceleration opportunities for gifted students throughout the schooling process is a basic right to an appropriate education, a key tenet in most school district mission statements. This book has suggested specific strategies for identifying candidates for acceleration, programmatic approaches to employ, curricular emphases, and specific teacher strategies to use for content acceleration in the classroom. It now concludes with a major plea for flexibility in placement procedures and the need for districtwide policies on acceleration to encourage a coherent response on the issue. School personnel need to be responsive to student needs by providing a set of acceleration options as basic education for these learners. To do less is to ignore 80 years of evidence of the success of acceleration with the gifted learner (Benbow & Lubinski, 1996).

Resources

Mathematics

Goldberg, H., & Wagreich, P. (1992–present). *Teaching integrated mathematics and science (TIMS).* Chicago: The University of Illinois at Chicago.

Greenes, C., Immerzeel , G., et al. (1997–1999). *Techniques of problem solving (TOPS).* Palo Alto, CA: Dale Seymour.

Jacobs, H. (1994). *Mathematics: A human endeavor* (3rd ed.). New York: Freeman.

Katzoff, S. *Twists and turns and tangles in math and physics.* Baltimore, MD: IAAY Publications and Resources, Johns Hopkins University.

National Council of Teachers of Mathematics (NCTM). (2001–2004). *Navigations: Steering through principles and standards* [series]. Retrieved March 30, 2004, from http://www.nctm.org/standards/navigations.htm

Serra, M. (1997). *Discovering geometry: An inductive approach* (2nd ed.). Emeryville, CA: Key Curriculum Press.

University of Chicago Mathematics Project (UCSMP). (2002). *Everyday mathematics* (2nd ed.). Chicago: The Wright Group.

Social Studies

Bank Street College Project in Science and Math. (1984–present). *The voyage of the Mimi.* Scotts Valley, CA: Wings for Learning.

Bruner, J. (1968). *Man: A course of study (MACOS).* Washington, DC: Education Development Center.

Center for Gifted Education. (2001). *College of William and Mary social studies units.* Dubuque, IA: Kendall/Hunt.

Gallagher, S. (n.d.). *PBLISS (Problem Based Learning in the Social Sciences).* Retrieved March 30, 2004, from http://www.uncc.edu/sagallag/pbliss/index.htm

Opposing viewpoints [Series]. San Diego, CA: Greenhaven Press.

Touchstone Discussions Project. (1993–2001). *Touchpebbles* [Series]. Philadelphia, PA: Research for Better Schools.

Language Arts

Center for Gifted Education. (1998–1999). *College of William and Mary language arts units.* Dubuque, IA: Kendall/Hunt.

Center for Gifted Education. (2003). *Navigator novel study guides.* Williamsburg, VA: Author. Retrieved March 30, 2004, from http://cfge.wm.edu/materials.php#Navigators

Junior Great Books [Series]. Chicago, IL: Great Books Foundation.

Seizer, J. (1991). *Conversations: Readings for writing.* New York: Macmillan.

Science

Biological Sciences Curriculum Study (BSCS). (1989–present). *Science for life and living.* Dubuque, IA: Kendall/Hunt.

Biological Sciences Curriculum Study (BSCS). (1996). *Biological science: A molecular approach* (BSCS Blue version, 7th ed.). Lexington, VA: Heath.

Center for Gifted Education. (1997). *College of William and Mary problem-based science units.* Dubuque, IA: Kendall/Hunt.

Education Development Center. (1991–present). *Insights: A hands-on elementary science curriculum.* Warren, NJ: Optical Data.

Foundational Approaches in Science Teaching (FAST). (1990). Honolulu: University of Hawaii: Curriculum Research and Development Group.

Jefferson County, CO, Public Schools. (1991). *Middle school of life science.* Dubuque, IA: Kendall/Hunt.

Lawrence Hall of Science. (1990–present). *Full option science system* (FOSS). Chicago: Encyclopedia Britannica Education Corp.

Lawrence Hall of Science. (1990–present). *Great explorations* in *math and science (GEMS).* Berkeley, CA: University of California.

References

Assouline, S. G., Colangelo, N., Lupkowski-Shoplik, A., Lipscomb, J. B., Forstadt, L. (2003). *Iowa Acceleration Scale 2nd edition manual: A guide for whole grade acceleration K–8.* Scottsdale, AR: Great Potential Press.

Benbow, C. P. (1991). Meeting the needs of gifted students through use of acceleration. In M. C. Wang, M. C. Reynolds, & H. J. Walberg (Eds.), *Handbook of special education* (Vol. 4, pp. 23–36). Elmsford, NY: Pergamon.

Benbow, C. P., & Lubinski, D. (1996). *Intellectual talent.* Baltimore, MD: Johns Hopkins University Press.

Benbow, C. P., & Stanley, J. C. (Eds.). (1983). *Academic precocity: Aspects of its development.* Baltimore, MD: Johns Hopkins University Press.

Brody, L., Assouline, S., & Stanley, J. (1990). Five years of early entrants: Predicting successful achievement in college. *Gifted Child Quarterly, 34*, 138–142.

Brody, L. E., & Benbow, C. P. (1987). Accelerative strategies: How effective are they for the gifted? *Gifted Child Quarterly, 3*, 105–110.

Brody, L. E., & Stanley, J. C. (1991). Young college students: Assessing factors that contribute to success. In W. T. Southern & E. D. Jones (Eds.), *Academic acceleration of gifted children* (pp. 102–132). New York: Teachers College Press.

Clark, B. (2002). *Growing up gifted: Developing the potential of children at home and at school* (6th ed.). Upper Saddle River, NJ: Prentice Hall.

Cornell, D., Callahan, C., & Loyd, B. (1991). Personality growth of female early college entrants: A controlled prospective study. *Gifted Child Quarterly, 35*, 135–143.

Daurio, S. P. (1979). Educational enrichment versus acceleration: A review of the literature. In W. C. George, S. J. Cohn, & J. C. Stanley (Eds.), *Educating the gifted: Acceleration and enrichment* (pp. 13–53). Baltimore, MD: Johns Hopkins University Press.

Elkind, D. (1981). *The hurried child: Growing up too fast too soon.* Newton, MA: Addison-Wesley.

Elkind, D. (1988). Mental acceleration. *Journal for the Education of the Gifted, 11*(4), 19–31.

Feldhusen, J. F., Proctor, T. B., & Black, K. N. (1986). Guidelines for grade advancement of precocious children. *Roeper Review, 9,* 25–27.

Gallagher, J. (1969). Gifted children. In R. L. Ebel (Ed.), *Encyclopedia of education research* (4th ed., pp. 537–544). New York: Macmillan.

Gallagher, J. J., & Gallagher, S. A. (1994). *Teaching the gifted child* (4th ed.). Boston: Allyn and Bacon.

Gross, M. U. M. (1994). Radical acceleration: Responding to academic and social needs of extremely gifted adolescents. *Journal of Secondary Gifted Education, 5*(4), 27–34.

Gross, M. U. M. (2004). *Exceptionally gifted children.* London: Routledge.

Gross, M. U. M., & van Vliet, H. E. (2003). *Radical acceleration of highly gifted children: An annotated bibliography of international research on highly gifted children who graduate from high school three or more years early*. Sydney, Australia: University of New South Wales.

Heinbokel, A. (2002). Acceleration: Still an option for the gifted. *Gifted Education International, 16,* 170–178.

Janos, P. M., Robinson, N., & Lunneborg, C. E. (1989). Markedly early entrance to college: A multi-year comparative study of academic performance and psychological adjustment. *Journal of Higher Education, 60,* 496–518.

Jones, E., & Southern, T. (1992). Programming, grouping, and acceleration in rural school districts: A survey of attitudes and practices. *Gifted Child Quarterly, 36,* 111–116.

Kulik, J. A., & Kulik, C. C. (1984). Synthesis of research on effects of accelerated instruction. *Educational Leadership, 42*(2), 84–89.

Kulik, J. A., & Kulik, C. C. (1992a). Meta-analytic findings on grouping programs. *Gifted Child Quarterly, 36,* 73–77.

Kulik, C. C., & Kulik, J. A. (1992b). Effects of ability grouping on secondary school students: A meta–analysis of evaluation findings. *American Educational Research Journal, 19,* 415–428.

Maddux, C. D., Stacy, D., & Scott, M. (1981). School entry age in a group of gifted children. *Gifted Child Quarterly, 4,* 180–183.

Marzano, R. (1999). *An analysis of national standards in relationship to instructional time.* Aurora, CO: McRel.

National Education Commission on Time and Learning. (1994). *Prisoners of time.* Washington, DC: U.S. Government Printing Office.

Obrzut, A., Nelson, R. B., & Obrzut, J. E. (1984). Early school entrance for intellectually superior children: An analysis. *Psychology in the Schools, 21*(1), 71–77.

Pressey, S. L. (1949). *Educational acceleration: Appraisal of basic problems* (Bureau of Educational Research Monographs No. 31). Columbus: Ohio State University Press.

Proctor, T. B., Black, K. N., & Feldhusen, J. F. (1986). Early admission of selected children to elementary school: A review of the literature. *Journal of Educational Research, 80*, 70–76.

Renzulli, J. S., Smith, L. H., & Reis, S. M. (1982). Curriculum compacting: An essential strategy for working with gifted students. *Elementary School Journal, 82,* 185–194.

Reynolds, M., Birch, J., & Tuseth, A. (1962). Review of research on early admission. In M. Reynolds (Ed.), *Early school admission for mentally advanced children* (pp. 7–18). Reston, VA: Council for Exceptional Children.

Richardson, T. M., & Benbow, C. P. (1990). Long-term effects of acceleration on the social-emotional adjustment of mathematically precocious youth. *Journal of Educational Psychology, 82*, 464–470.

Robinson, N., & Janos, P. (1986). Psychological adjustment in a college-level program of marked academic acceleration. *Journal of Youth and Adolescence, 15*, 51–60.

Schiever, S. W., & Maker, C. J. (1997). Enrichment and acceleration: An overview and new directions. In N. Colangelo & G. A. Davis (Eds.), *Handbook of gifted education* (2nd ed., pp. 113–125). Boston: Allyn and Bacon.

Southern, T., & Jones, E. (Eds.). (1991). *The academic acceleration of gifted children.* New York: Teachers College Press.

Stanley, J. C. (1979). The study and facilitation of talent for mathematics. In A. H. Passow (Ed.), *The gifted and talented: Their education and development* (pp. 169–185). Chicago: University of Chicago Press.

Swiatek, M. A., & Benbow, C. P. (1991a). Effects of fast-paced mathematics courses on the development of mathematically precocious students. *Journal of Research in Mathematics Education, 22*, 139–150.

Swiatek, M. A., & Benbow, C. P. (1991b). Ten-year longitudinal follow-up of ability-matched accelerated and unaccelerated gifted students. *Journal of Educational Psychology, 83,* 528–538.

Terman, L., & Oden, M. H. (1947). *The gifted child grows up: Twenty-five years' follow-up of a superior group.* Stanford, CA: Stanford University Press.

VanTassel-Baska, J. (1986). Acceleration. In J. Maker (Ed.),

Critical issues in gifted education (pp. 179–196). Rockville, MD: Aspen.

VanTassel-Baska, J. (1996). Contributions of the talent-search concept to gifted education. In C. P. Benbow & D. Lubinski (Eds.), *Intellectual talent* (pp. 236–245). Baltimore, MD: Johns Hopkins University Press.

VanTassel-Baska, J. (2003). *Curriculum planning and instructional design for gifted learners.* Denver: Love.

VanTassel-Baska, J. (2004). Quo vadis? Laboring in the classical vineyards: An optimal challenge for gifted secondary students. *Journal of Secondary Gifted Education, 15,* 56–60.

VanTassel-Baska, J., & Little, C. (Eds.). (2003). *Content-based curriculum for high-ability learners.* Waco, TX: Prufrock Press.

VanTassel-Baska, J., & Olszewski-Kubilius, P. (Eds.). (1988). *Patterns of influence on gifted learners: The home, the self, and the school.* New York: Teachers College Press.

VanTassel-Baska, J., Patton, J., & Prillaman, P. (1991). *Gifted youth at risk: A report of a national study.* Reston, VA: Council for Exceptional Children.

Walberg, H. J., & Reynolds, M. C. (Eds.). (1994). *Handbook of special and remedial education: Research and practice.* St. Louis, MO: Elsevier.

About the Author

Joyce VanTassel-Baska is The Jody and Layton Smith Professor of Education and executive director of the Center for Gifted Education at the College of William and Mary, where she has developed a graduate program and a research and development center in gifted education. Dr. VanTassel-Baska has published widely, including 15 books and more than 275 refereed journal articles, book chapters, and scholarly reports. She also serves as the editor of *Gifted and Talented International*, a publication of the World Council on Gifted and Talented. Dr. VanTassel-Baska has received numerous awards for her work, including the National Association for Gifted Children's Early Leader Award in 1986, the State Council of Higher Education in Virginia Outstanding Faculty Award in 1993, the Phi Beta Kappa faculty award in 1995, and the National Association of Gifted Children Distinguished Scholar Award in 1997. She was selected as a Fulbright Scholar to New Zealand in 2000 and a visiting scholar to Cambridge University in England in 1993. Her major research interests are on the talent development process and effective curricular interventions with the gifted.

Printed in the United States
by Baker & Taylor Publisher Services